T0300427

ISO 9001 and Lean

Friends, Not Foes, For Providing Efficiency and Customer Value

ISO 9001 and Lean

Friends, Not Foes, For Providing Efficiency and Customer Value

Douglas Meyer

Routledge
Taylor & Francis Group

A PRODUCTIVITY PRESS BOOK

First edition published in 2019
by Routledge/Productivity Press
52 Vanderbilt Avenue, 11th Floor New York, NY 10017
2 Park Square, Milton Park, Abingdon, Oxon OX14 4RN, UK

International Standard Book Number-13: 978-0-367-18824-5 (Paperback)
978-0-367-13715-1 (Hardback)

Library of Congress Cataloging-in-Publication Data

Names: Meyer, Douglas, author.
Title: ISO 9001 and lean : friends, not foes, for providing efficiency and customer value / Douglas Meyer.
Description: New York, NY : Routledge, 2019. | Includes bibliographical references and index.
Identifiers: LCCN 2018054014 (print) | LCCN 2018057484 (ebook) | ISBN 9780429028243 (e-Book) | ISBN 9780367188245 (pbk. : alk. paper) | ISBN 9780367137151 (hardback : alk. paper)
Subjects: LCSH: ISO 9001 standard. | Lean manufacturing. | Quality control. | Customer relations.
Classification: LCC TS156.6 (ebook) | LCC TS156.6 .M486 2019 (print) | DDC 658.4/013--dc23
LC record available at https://lccn.loc.gov/2018054014

Visit the Taylor & Francis Web site at
http://www.taylorandfrancis.com

Contents

Preface

Let's face reality. Literature describing the glorious virtues of Lean Manufacturing sounds so inviting and practical, one can hardly imagine anyone in the manufacturing community wanting to disregard an interest in reducing waste or engaging employees, saving money, or doing a Kaizen event, especially when it is in a foreign language.

On the other hand, after several decades of rather challenging implementation in factories, the risk is much higher for many in the manufacturing community to have jaded perspectives on the true value and a clear understanding of the proper implementation of Lean and its systems and tools. Many have made several runs at it, with very mixed results. Theoretically, and from top management's perspective, there is little to no debate that it simply needs to be done. It fits so beautifully with reducing costs and making profit. What about that doesn't make cents? (pun intended).

But I wrote this book for a specific purpose.

During my more than 30 years of manufacturing leadership experience in different companies and countries, I have grown to appreciate the passionate support of quality professionals in pursuit of excellence in manufacturing despite the challenge of the human–machine interface, including, of course, the human emotion, opinion, and character variances.

I have seen a wide variety of attitudes toward ISO-controlled environments, but with proper leadership, these environments have proven to be exceptional systems to maintain the integrity of the manufacturing processes.

With the increasing global competitive nature of manufacturing, I have also seen an ever-growing interest in driving continuous improvement within the manufacturing community. Having a culture of listening and developing our most important asset—our people—is utterly important and certainly a respectful way to lead. However, engaging all employees in this improvement strategy increases the opportunity for processes within manufacturing to be adjusted without a full comprehension of the interconnectedness of those adjustments.

In many places, Lean is not a "clearly" controlled process. It's flexible, engaging, and intended to emphasize the value that people bring to the improvement process. However, that wonderful creativity and mindset must be in perfect collaboration with controlled processes and corresponding documentation around them. Many sites don't fully grasp the depth of this statement. Additionally, it is not always fully supported by all levels of the organization.

Hence, there tends to be a rather significant gap between empowering people and controlling the processes. I have often reflected on my reading the work of an excellent author, Eliyahu H. Goldratt, and specifically his book *The Goal*. During one point in my career, I even gave my manufacturing employees time off task to read the book during work hours. And, as a result, I had the joy of helping our most important factory workers understand and buy in to something that didn't sound too interesting—the Theory of Constraints.

In this same light, I hope to inspire readers to help their people understand how to create sustainable, auditable, and continuous improvement. Not with a textbook; not with an academic, statistically significant, analytical book; and not with a Power Pointless presentation. I consider it most appropriate and effective to get this gap in understanding filled in a simple "manufacturing story" format. An honest, real-life story that points out how we can truly tie improvement and sustainability of those improvement systems and improvement ideas together through controlled documentation. They should be the best of friends.

ISO 9001:2015 creates the framework for continuous improvement, and this book shows a real-life story of how it can truly work, with questions at the end of each chapter to spur the customized solution you can implement to remain competitive and, hopefully, have more fun.

I hope you enjoy the read.

Author

With more than 30 years in manufacturing, **Douglas Meyer** has had the privilege to work for three different Fortune 500 companies, with an array of leadership roles in most all areas of manufacturing, engineering, purchasing, and supply chain operations, including more than five years of landed experience in mainland China. With a Bachelor of Science in Industrial Engineering and a Master of Science in Industrial Manufacturing Systems Engineering, he has been fortunate to be able to implement systems and tools in a wide variety of industries—automotive, electrical/electronics, film, industrial, medical, and bio-processing. Clearly, improving processes in a controlled manner in these industries is utterly essential.

Whether as third-shift Supervisor in a Union environment inspiring his team to enthusiastically implement the Theory of Constraints, as Manufacturing Manager driving plant layout and one-piece flow, as Supply Chain Manager implementing factory worker visibility and leadership of inventory conditions in each warehouse, or as Vice President opening up a greenfield ISO-13485 manufacturing site in a foreign land, he knows the value of employee engagement combined well with a system that helps make sure that the integrity of our defined processes is maintained.

Doug is a native Iowan, an avid fan of StrengthsFinder for more than 20 years, a professional photographer, a cancer survivor, and a Christ follower. Doug has had leadership roles in a variety of other institutions, including church planting and eldership, and is a husband and father of a biracial family with three wonderful children.

1

AOP: Acronym-O-Phobia

Herein begins the story of a team of manufacturing employees committed to serving their customers with top quality products in the most cost effective way in order to help their organization succeed. Manufacturing requires strong leadership, empowered employees, and increasingly efficient, controlled processes. Sound simple? Read on.

"How in the world do you think we should handle all of this new age thinking on empowerment and engagement?" asked Janice as she scratched her head in her normal fashion when anything new came out of the Lean department. "You'd think that we don't need boards and Post-it® Notes to follow up on concerns, since we already have notebooks, emails, bulletin boards, meetings, and then our normal work order system that's pretty easy to log into."

"What do you mean, new age thinking?" asked Doug. "We've been 'suggesting' a suggestion box for more than 30 years. Don't you realize that all we're trying to do is to make the suggestion box more visible and actually demonstrate that we truly care about our employees' ideas? Then, of course, we want to get them engaged in the solution!"

Janice responds, "Well then, are you saying that the new terms around here—empowerment and engagement—are our new vocabulary for actually paying attention to people who add value to our organization? We've always done that! In fact, the last

DOESN'T STAND FOR ANYTHING

time that I checked, our Production leadership has no locks on their cubicles or doors and there is no service fee for going to talk to anyone around here. So, why do you call it 'new'?"

"Not so fast with that assumption," Doug replied. "We all know how much we care about our employees when we call them by that precious acronym FTEs. Full-time equivalents? Do you think that's empowering? We go through more management fads around here than a tabloid newspaper has stories for Big Foot. It's time we actually started to get serious about what we do here. Or would you rather just be an average Joe in the world of work force reductions and outsourcing? We need to really show some integrity around here. We are constantly broadcasting that our employees are our most valuable asset, yet when they come up with an idea, we simply don't listen. We really don't. We get back into that mode of always seeing people as wanting to complain, wanting the work to not be…. work."

Janice is rather bothered by Doug's whole arrogant statement. In her world, it often appears that the Lean department is simply creating waste, not removing it. Waste in rebranding a system that has been tried 10 times before, now has a new acronym, and is spoken of like it is the greatest thing since sliced bread. "We are never opposed to good ideas, Doug. Everyone, at least in the Production departments, understands the metrics and knows we always must do more with less. If it isn't TPM, it's TQM or VDM or DMAIC or PDCA or some other new way of saying we are rebranding the old way of saying we must work smarter, not faster. We put in time every day, all day, usually about 11 hours a day, simply trying to make sure that we meet our goals and satisfy our customers. We get new problems popping up every day and hardly have time to document each one and make sure it never comes back. It is simply not that easy. We know we need to improve. We hear it from management, we hear it from Quality, and we hear it from HR. All of them are paid solely on what *we* produce, NOT on what *they* produce. Most of the departments in our organization are made up of good people, but they sometimes lose sight of the fact that without producing a part, we don't satisfy the customer, we don't create revenue, and they don't have a job! Oh, how I wish that everyone could really see how important my employees are, and how rebranding something 'empowerment' or a Lean Management System isn't enough, when all along we know it is simply the next regurgitated management theory someone pulled out of a Business Strategy book. That, my friend, is simply bogus. It won't work with my employees. They are smarter than that. I only wish everyone else realized it. Not only are they smart, but they are also the ones that make product for us. And, if I might add, for our families!"

Door SLAMs! Mike Gurlack enters Janice's quaint glassed-in office and interrupts the lingering silence after Janice's soliloquy on the value of people. "Where in the heck is Norton!? I've been paging him for more than 5 minutes and it seems he must be more interested in reading his social media ticker than he is in getting the yoke machine to run! Doesn't he realize that his job is not to be the HR representative for all his Twitter fans, but to actually come out and fix the equipment when we are down and Bilher #4 needs parts?!"

Janice looks squarely at Doug in a manner that communicates clearly "see, I told you so" and goes out to pursue solving this next emergency drill. "So, Doug, when you get a chance, post something for me in regards to celebrating another empowered manager going out to save the day from the evils of one of the 7 deadly wastes—machine idle time…." What a poignant comment thrown across the bow of Doug's attempt to convince Janice to implement his new Lean Manufacturing System (LMS).

The door closes behind Mike and Janice. Doug is left alone in the aquarium-like office, swimming by himself. He knows how important it is to engage employees. He knows how the principle of "Seeking First to Understand, Then Be Understood" truly is the right way. But he simply can't figure out how to resolve the issue of the "tyranny of the urgent" in the midst of employee engagement and empowerment. It's a manufacturing conundrum that needs a solution. When we talk about making sure that all employees are involved in the process of continuous improvement, we can easily get a little glassy-eyed. Doug understands how some people like to immediately discount a new idea, sometimes because they have been jaded by so many past experiences that end up going down a dead-end pathway. They aren't interested in jumping on board with any new fad. They aren't interested in jumping into any program sponsored by the PLT (Plant Leadership Team). They know it always takes boots on the ground to make sure whatever the PLT says really gets accomplished. If leadership doesn't go to the "Gemba," they don't get it…. Hmmm….

"Did I just mention the term Gemba?" he thinks to himself. "Why do we want to call it a Gemba? Isn't it better to simply state that I am going to go out to the floor, to the place where value is created, and see what is going on?" Just then, production employee Jim Bouges comes into the office. He seems eager to talk about something.

"Hey, have you seen Janice?" he asks. "Yeah, she just went out to Bilher #4 to see if she could help get support there to get it up and running," Doug replies. "Oh," he musters. "I just wanted to check with her on what to do about our new team starting to 5S the Bilher #2 machine. It seems like everyone is excited to work on it, but we got into a big argument about how many S's are really part of the project. It seems like Ron wants to add a sixth S, and Sharon wants to even add a seventh S. We spent so much time talking about how many S's we need, we didn't even get to explain what we really need to do. Everyone knows how important it is to keep the sensors clean, given how Mary almost got hurt when she was trying to clean the machine without knowing all the safety rules. So, I had heard that we had this new Lean guy in the organization, and I recognized your picture from the email announcement. I suspect you know all the acronyms and can help our team get back on track. That's why I stopped in." "Well," Doug said, "That sounds like a real dilemma you and your team got into. I wonder why in the world people do such things. Why don't they just let it slide by and get back to business and getting the project done? Are we creating this situation? What do you think?" By the way, Doug had recently heard that the Japanese had managed to Lean the 5S process down to only 3S's. Now, that sounds like a Lean idea!

"I am not sure I can answer the question for everyone, Doug, but for myself, I think we have spent too much time and energy teaching people new buzzwords and acronyms. Every time we get a new manager or a new Lean guy, they all seem to want to put their own slant on things. They own their new job and want to be seen as a leader. They want to talk in the latest politically correct manufacturing speak. It seems rather trite to me. To us on the floor, we don't need another three-letter description of common sense and we certainly don't need to use another language to describe things that mean 'getting out and finding out what is really going on.' In fact, most of the time that type of 'management speak' turns us off almost immediately.

If there is anything good we could say about it, it's that it gives us something to talk about at lunch!"

"Really?" Doug mused, "I understand that this is certainly your view point, but you are definitely implying that this is more like a general consensus out there. After you put it so bluntly, which I thank you for, I truly get what you are trying to say. We get paid more to talk in a foreign language so that we might persuasively convince you that we are educated and professional and that we should use big words so we sound that way, right?"

"Yep, that is the frustrating part about new acronyms and new theories. They are simply rewrapped common sense. They don't do what you really want them to do: Help the people. Now, don't get me wrong, I like this company and I am glad I have a job, so I can go home and put food on the table. It's just that calling it 5S or 6S or even 7S simply doesn't matter to me. I know we need a cleaner machine and a properly maintained machine and a good amount of spare parts. I have no idea how many S's that adds up to. But you have the Manufacturing Engineer and the Supply Chain Analyst, who have never cleaned a machine in their lives here, hotly debating the value of two extra S's. Are you kidding me?!"

"By the way, what is your name?" Doug asks. "Jim. Jim Bouges." "OK, Jim, give me your schedule and I will join you at the next meeting. I am sure we can make some better progress, after that coaching session you gave me just now. Besides, I agree with you on the importance of properly maintaining our equipment. I look forward to doing what I can to support you. But, one last question: Do you know much I appreciated your transparency and willingness to provide me feedback?" Jim pauses a little, and then says, "Well, if you can get us off the ABW, I would sure appreciate it." "Huh?" Doug quickly responds, as he really has no clue what Jim is talking about. "You know. The Acronym Band Wagon!"

Got it, Jim. Thanks. I look forward to seeing you again.

By the time this conversation is over Janice is heading back into the office. She isn't smiling, and it doesn't look pretty. "Are you still removing waste?" she says under her breath as she steps into the office and heads immediately for the phone. It isn't hard to tell her sense of urgency is remaining as high as when she went out to Bilher #4. She calls and discusses her views on how things are going at the machine with whoever has the pleasure of talking with her. Doug pauses to attempt to capture the meaning of the conversation he had with Jim, as well as the rather dynamic, almost impulsive behavior of Janice.

When it comes down to how complicated the manufacturing process is, Doug has reason to believe that there is some form of continuous improvement that could take place here. There doesn't appear to be a smooth and logical process in place that people support and get behind. The general population is probably yearning to support common sense. But, as Doug remembers from an Eliyahu Goldratt quote, "common sense is not so common."

Doug realizes that it is time to head off to his next meeting. A meeting to discuss the ISO External Audit Report. Yes, another acronym. Another opportunity to learn why people behave the way they do. Yet this one, strangely enough, has an acronym that seems to be stable. It seems to have an air of reasonableness. As far as Doug can remember, ISO has been a certification process that is respected in the industry as a standard system that makes sure you make products that are safe, reliable, and of good quality. And, requires documented evidence that you do what you say you do.

Doug can't wait to discuss how the continuous improvement system can be positively influenced by the Quality Management System. He eagerly heads off to this next meeting.

Actions and Discussion Points	Longer-Term Actions
Write down as many acronyms as you can in 10 minutes.	Create and/or update a *Site Acronym Dictionary*.
Discuss the pros and cons of acronyms. Pros: Cons:	Properly manage the *Dictionary* for maximum productivity.
Discuss the value of using foreign words to describe actions being taken.	Properly create useful *Dictionary of Approved Foreign Words*.
Discuss ways to improve communication.	

2

"Can adding an additional Management System really be Lean?"

— Douglas R. Meyer, ISO 9001 and Lean

The Real Issue

Doug dawdles down to the Quality department, eager to step into the meeting with a fresh perspective on helping people. He has always appreciated the Quality department but, quite frankly, the range of employees in the Quality department at Square M's seems to be rather slim. Perhaps that relates to the actual role of an effective Quality person. Doug realizes that the Quality department has the role of saying "No." This is not always an easy thing to do when the Production leadership wants to make sure the parts are approved and shipped for an urgently needed customer order. Everyone wants to work together and do the right things, but the quality role must stand in the crosshairs of customer delivery and appropriate product quality. To make matters worse, in the world of manufacturing, the line of good quality can sometimes be a little blurry. Of course, it is true that there are prints and specifications and all the detail one would ever want behind these written documents. There are also allowances when things don't quite meet the requirements of the part specification but are still acceptable for a customer. The deviations from standard are dependent on many variables, but surely the Quality department has a big part in the final say of what gets shipped and what does not get shipped. So, when Doug thinks about the narrow range of Quality department people, he does so with a reasonable amount of respect. Howie Shears, for example, is one of the best employees in the department and always negotiates diplomatically with everyone on a good solution to the gray area that originally caused the discussion with the Quality department. He is a logical, process thinker who uses a combination of good, practical engineering knowledge together with a strong dose of common sense. Unfortunately, he is not always the main contact for every product in the facility. Don Salles, on the other hand, is the kind of guy that would simply prefer to make you suffer. He has no interest in your perspective and only wants to adhere to the letter of the law—the actual specifications; and, I might add, as only he sees them. There is no need for discussion with him, because he simply doesn't want to budge. In fact, it almost appears like he enjoys telling people "no." Why do people like this exist in manufacturing? Why do they tend to gravitate to the Quality department? Doug thinks the answer is obvious. Their natural propensity to be stubborn fits well with the role of maintaining outgoing quality. They realize that customer perception and customer satisfaction is related to the ability to support the agreement to send them product that meets the agreed upon dimensions and characteristics. They are not interested in product recalls, angry customers, or bad media coverage on the quality of the products. They feel very proud of what they stand for and how important their stubbornness can be. So, yes, the gravitational pulls of particular types of people make it easy to understand that the range is thin. Doug knows that, even before heading into the meeting.

"Are we all here?" Mike Watmoor asks as he kicks off the meeting. "As usual, Dave Hilmes is not here yet, but I think we can start without him," Janice calls out as she herself finally arrives and takes a seat at the table. "I have him working over at Bilher #1 trying to get it up and running, and he said he is almost done. So, why don't we go ahead?" "OK," Mike starts off, "we have good news to report. We had no findings in our ISO external audit. Isn't that great!?" "What do you mean by 'no findings'?" Doug asks. "Because it seems to me that, from my experience, we have plenty of areas that we could improve."

Sensing the Lean slant on the comment, Mike responds, "Doug, thank you for the spirit of continuous improvement in that question. As we all well know, there are always many ways an organization can improve, but when it comes to our external ISO auditor findings, we must realize that success is rooted in the sustainability of our ISO certification, not in this particular organization attempting to micromanage our continuous improvement processes and how well we are all doing in every aspect of our business. Last time I checked, I think that is more in your area of expertise…." Ouch, Doug thinks. This is not the type of answer he was expecting from a top level Quality Manager. Laying all that aside, at least in verbal form, Doug pursues the intent of his original request. "So, what you are saying is that the auditor didn't find any nonconformities, right?" "That's right," chimes in Dan Salles, Doug's favorite black-is-black and white-is-white Quality technician. "I think we did another excellent job this year, which makes it eight years in a row with no nonconformities. While I think you like to oppose my tough stance on our product quality here at Square M's, Doug, I think the record proves that our department understands its mission and gets the job done. We realize we aren't gods, but we do value the strength we possess in making sure the Production group doesn't get out of control and cause us a real problem."

Whoa! Doug wonders if that is the definition of empowerment, or simply a display of arrogant, irrational attitudes about what keeps a company in a truly competitive position with all the other companies that make similar product. "So, tell me, Dan, what is the real purpose of our ISO certification? Is it to make sure we always make good product or is it that we always stretch to improve ourselves to improve our company, take market share, and provide stable successful employment for our employees under the guidance of our standards and specifications?"

"Well, so glad you can voice your opinion, Doug," Mike mentions. "The reality of business is clear. We need our ISO certification to remain intact, and we need to make sure we don't screw anything up." Sensing a form of management that doesn't seem to fully understand the value of what is offered, Doug asks, "So, then, what is the real result of the findings? Did we get any observations or, heaven forbid, any praise or noteworthy notes?"

"Well, finally a question I'm glad you asked," Mike continues. "We did have two observations, both of which relate to minor issues in calculations related to Cpk in our molding of the encasements. Ryan is already looking into it and we should be able to make some little tweaks to improve the situation and minimize the risk during the next audit. I was very happy to see how well Ryan responded to the observations. He really seemed to understand their point. I will follow up on both of the issues next week and see if I can close them out in our internal documents." "But wait just a second," Doug cautions, "seeing as you don't particularly appreciate my commentary, I think I will voice another concern here. Molding has had that same issue for years and we have come to the conclusion that everything we tweak in there only creates more waste and more variation. I realize that the variation is still within specification, but why don't we pay attention to what Sheila Bazel said over a year ago? It seems like we would rather take the easy route and just tweak something rather than take on the task of really improving the process. I know she's not an engineer and she's not your favorite mold operator, but the truth of the matter is that she has a ton of common sense and she tells it like it is. Will Ryan go talk to her?" "Not sure," Mike says, "but you can feel free to take that as a personal action item. In fact, if you want you can even post it on one of your new LMS boards if you want!"

Doug, noticeably impacted by the snideness of the comment, agrees to follow up with both Ryan and Sheila, both people who Doug feels very comfortable talking to. But he decides to forgive Mike's attitude and continues to attempt to make progress, using his most prepared explanation of the ISO standard as it relates to continuous improvement. "So, I will surely follow up with them to see what we can do, but, correct me if I am wrong, doesn't the ISO 9001:2008 Section 8.5.1 state explicitly that the Quality Management System is to be improved through the use of quality policy, quality objectives, audit results, analysis of data, corrective and preventative actions, and management review? Now, I realize that this is not carried over in the new 2015 standard, but they do mention that the results of analysis and evaluation from clause 9.1.3 and the outputs of management review from clause 9.3 are to be considered for needs or opportunities that must be addressed as part of continual improvement, right?"

The entire crowd is in shock. The silence in the room borders on deafening. Several people look at each other as if to see if anyone has a good comeback to Doug's seemingly prepared statement.

Doug continues, "The real issue is not 'did we maintain our certification?', although that in itself is a worthy goal. The real issue is 'if we have a standard that doesn't drive us to continually improve our quality and product for our customer, then what will keep us in business?' Of course, don't get me wrong, I realize that any change to the organization carries with it an issue of risk management. Or speaking in normal language, if we change something, what is the benefit compared to the cost of the change? Who has the freedom to change something around here? How do we manage change? How do we leverage all our employees' brains to make sure we get better without the risk of creating problems for our customers? Or, putting it as bluntly as I possibly can, how do we create a culture of continuous improvement in the midst of an ISO system that has a goal to keep things as standardized and stable as possible?"

Dan decides to take a stab at this: "Aha, do you really trust that all those people out there know what they can change and when they can change it and how much risk they are throwing into our system by simply thinking they have a good idea? Are you out of your Lean Management System mind?! No wonder they call you Lean. I think that correlates with the measure of gray matter between your two ears! We can't just go changing everything willy-nilly. This company's product has a great reputation in the industry. But it can cause serious injury and damage if we don't control our processes! So, in answer to anything you offer, I do think it needs to go through a controlled process. Control is not a negative word. It keeps us from doing something stupid, creates a lot less risk for our lawyers to have to deal with, and sets the tone for the entire company that we don't produce junk!"

Doug takes a deep breath and works hard to seek first to understand and then, and only then, be understood. "I understand that you have noble values for the cause of Square M's, so let me attempt to rephrase what you said in my own words and see if you agree. Your valid point is that we have a quality system that we all own and we all must subscribe to, but that at times like these, we are not exactly prepared to handle a flood of 'good ideas' from our valued employees without some form of system that effectively manages the risk. Does that hit the nail on the head?" Both Mike and Dan agree and say in unison, "Yep!"

"Well, now we are getting somewhere. Because, as our dear friend Albert Einstein once stated, the definition of insanity is "doing the same thing over and over again and expecting different results."

If we as an organization have any chance of survival, we must be able to do more with less. Our Quality Management System has documented to all of us that we need to evaluate our management review for ways to drive our continuous improvement. Always saying no to change is like always saying no to progress. Now, I get that every change doesn't necessarily result in progress. That is clearly your point, Dan, and I definitely don't want to make light of that. However, that being said, why don't we march down a path where we consider ISO documentation as a method of continually improving our business?"

Mike thinks for a while, and then says, "Hmm… I like the idea. Just not quite sure how risky it would be to add a bunch of Post-it® Notes to our certification documentation…. Let's contemplate this for a while. Besides, our time is up, and most of us have another meeting."

The group disbands, leaving Doug rather disheartened.

The real issue is: We have two management systems—a Lean Management System and an ISO Quality Management System—and it seems that these two management systems have different objectives. But Doug thinks to himself, … . "Why can't they work together?"

Actions and Discussion Points
Describe the current relationship between the Lean and Quality organization.
Contemplate the reason for the need for two management systems. Pros: Cons:
Consider having one management system. What steps would need to be taken?

3

ISO What?

Mike leaves the room of the ISO External Audit briefing with mixed emotions; excited about how well the audit went, confused by people's lack of enthusiasm, and eager to contemplate what the differences are between the two systems and what in the world Square M's should do about it. Mike, an introvert by nature, starts to think about whether he needs to call a meeting about this topic and discuss it with everyone. His mind wanders back to the initial startup of the ISO system and how proud of it everyone seemed to be. While it is clearly communicated through the sales channels and in marketing that the company has this certification, he really isn't sure if it is a competitive advantage any longer. He doesn't care so much about whether it does or does not make a difference, but his curiosity has been aroused. Besides, these days everyone has this certification, so it doesn't provide much differentiation.

Regardless of this thought, he is in favor of the value of the Quality Management System and is a strong advocate of anything ISO. It does seem to get everyone in the plant on one system. That is what confuses him. The Lean department just came in and decided that they can have their own system to improve the place and that there needs to be no control over any of "their" documents.

He decides to first bring up the External Audit at the Plant Manager's staff meeting and see if any of the other managers have any other perspective on the value of the ISO system, before cracking the whip on adding more documents to the relatively succinct system. That meeting is scheduled for later in the afternoon, so he prepares himself mentally for the discussion while he hopes, deep inside, that people have good responses to the value of the certification.

In the meantime, Doug has stepped out of that challenging situation into another one—right out onto the production floor at Bilher #1, which is still not running very well. Kelly, the Bilher #1 Operator, rather impatiently speaks up, "What is going on here, Doug?" Doug replies with willful intent, "What do you mean?" "Surely you jest, Doug," Kelly replies, "I certainly can't forget the last monthly meeting where you were expressing the virtues of empowerment and engagement. But out here, people think you don't have a clue when you seem to want to run bad parts! I think that we have a controlled document here that states clearly what I am not supposed to run, and I think we should stick to it. Call me a radical, but when I read our Quality policy on the back of my employee card, I think it means that when we set policies, we should follow them; not for the sake of being stubborn, but for the sake of doing what is right for the customer. I get the reality of how some dimensions and some issues are simply in the gray area of manufacturing life, but I can't really make up my own quality policy. If the parts aren't in spec, they aren't in spec. If the spec is wrong, we need to fix it. If we don't have time to fix the spec, I need a deviation from the standard to run the parts. It's as simple as that."

Doug stands in awe of what he just heard. After coming out of a rather depressing meeting about the value of maintaining a standard for the sake of the customer and your own reputation, Doug sees that Kelly has a real sense of value as it relates to the standard. His objection to running on wrong specs is pure. He isn't throwing out acronyms and buzzwords and trying to create a scene. He is simply trying to make sure that he doesn't pass along poor quality to the next work station. A work station, I might add, that desperately needs more parts.

What more could Doug ask for from an employee? What more could the ISO registrations mean to an employee? Why is it so hard to see the value of disciplined control over *all* processes?

"Shut down the machine," Doug says, "I will take the heat on this one." Kelly, rather shocked by the initiative of Doug, says, "Sounds good, boss. I will head off to see Mike Harns in the tool room and see if we can't get this problem taken care of. If Janice comes by, tell her where I took off to. Thanks."

Doug pauses to reflect on the decision he made and hopes, with a reasonable measure of confidence, that that lesson in empowerment will be seen as one more step toward a culture that demonstrates that people really do matter. Empowerment is not giving people power. It's simply allowing them to utilize their experience to make decisions with the power they have already.

But then Doug ponders, "What does that mean for our Lean Management System? Are we really serious about it? Do we have people on the floor that buy into it like Kelly did? Do we really understand what we are doing when it comes to Lean?" All good questions that come from the bright shining moment of someone believing in a standard.

"Hey, what's going on here? Where's Kelly?" Janice yells as she arrives at the 'scene of the crime.' "Oh, he did a great job of 'doing his job' by going to the tool room to get Mike and have him properly adjust the tool rather than limping on the edge of the gray zone and potentially creating problems downstream at Bilher #4," Doug says. "He mentioned the new controlled document Quality Alert and wanted to make sure his team was helping him get the process under control. He may not be a big fan of acronyms, but he sure likes having the Cpk, the capability of the process to remain in specification, in working order, so he can live with himself and stand by the Quality policy we all agreed to live by."

Janice, knowing that Doug is supporting the very premise of her argument earlier, graciously obliges and heads back to the fish tank office and the joy of being a full-time manufacturing manager. Doug, on the other hand, internally satisfied at getting the approval, waits patiently for Mike to make the proper adjustments to the tool, with Kelly's advice, and chalks this up as one small example of helping people manage decisions based on standards. He feels a little wasteful sitting there watching them work on the machine, but he knows the lingering will have some bearing on the learning process.

He, for the first time in his short career as the Lean Manager, realizes that the same passion and support for quality standards demonstrated by one guy at one machine is rarely, if ever, demonstrated by those people he has asked, or shall we say, required, to "implement" the Lean Management System.

Why?

There does seem to be something missing. Doug is not quite ready to throw out a thesis, but he is warming up to the need to link Section 10 of 9001:2015 with the process that he himself is dismally implementing.

Actions and Discussion Points
Describe the current ISO control of the existing Lean Management System at your site.
Briefly sketch out or find a pictorial showing the history of Lean at your site.
Describe how you "think" the factory workers view this history and process.
How does this impact your critical thinking? How does it align with common sense?

4

Lean on Me, When You're Not Strong

Doug is not strong.

He has seen the implementation of his Lean Management System process flounder. Surely, there are pockets of success, but overall, the implementation isn't going well. Some people really like the idea and support it, while others constantly make fun of it and just consider it another example of how management participates in an expensive management training course and comes back and tries to implement, whatever they learned until they decide to move onto the next latest fad or acronym.

Quite honestly, the process seems robust, but the application is lacking zeal and follow-through. What Doug's management has been most concerned about is the vicious circle for him. And, yes, it has him quite confused.

"So, Doug, how are things going for our new LMS?" asks Jamie, the Plant Manager at the weekly Plant Manager's staff meeting. "Well, overall pretty well," Doug replies, somewhat cautiously, "We had 145 suggestions logged from our employees last week, which really shows how many important things they have to say. We closed out about 53 of them, and we are comfortable with that progress and how we are continually improving. We can't say enough about how empowered our employees feel about the new system." "Really?" Tim Kech, the Financial Manager pipes in, "With fixing this many issues, you would think that our production numbers would be going through the roof.

Unfortunately, that is simply not the case. In fact, last week was one of our worst weeks this year. Now, I get that corrective actions don't always show results right away, but at the same time, I see we have a lot of off-task meetings out there and a lot less production coming out of the pipelines. In fact, Bilher #1 has been down a good part of the day, and this creates a real problem for us to get those orders out to the West Coast warehouse by end of day tomorrow. I just want to make sure we aren't all excited about a silly metric related to Post-it® Notes and not concerned about those folks that buy our product—that is if we have some for them to buy…."

Doug, somewhat appreciative and somewhat annoyed about these comments, responds, "Tim, I realize that what you are saying is quite true. We don't want to create a system that reports on what we got done with the LMS system that doesn't tie into real benefit." "I'm glad you brought that up," Mike chimes in, "From a quality perspective, I am not even sure of which changes have been made and what impact that will have on our risk mitigation related to the changes. How in the world do you propose we make sure that we didn't just change something that drives our system the wrong way? What if the great idea someone just had creates the need for a recall of all our products? Surely, we can empower our people, as I have heard you eloquently proclaim, but doesn't there need to be a check and balance for all this activity? Am I the only one worried about this, or is everyone else simply claiming the typical quality paranoia syndrome for me again?"

"Well, now that you mention paranoia," Todd joins in, "We engineers have certain reasons why we design machines the way we do, and sometimes we feel that the more we let every FTE we've got in this building break rank and start tweaking things, the better chance we have that Bilher #1 will be down all week! We designed our systems with a focused, process-minded logic. We don't just wing it and hope all is well. After all, our product is a safety device, and, heaven forbid, we should get into such a situation that someone was asleep at the wheel of controlling our process and continuous improvement turns into continuous lawsuits! Quite frankly, I don't think we are all on the same page with this new system of yours, Doug. I think the roll out was sexy, and the boards look really nice out there, but the fact that whenever I run by one of them and see that they are not up to date shows our lack of follow-up in our organization, and that simply doesn't impress me, or, I'm guessing, anyone else, for that matter."

Doug cringes at the use of the "full-time equivalent" acronym but decides to let it slide… this time. "Anyone else want to pile on? I mean, add other comments?"

"Well, yes, now that you ask, I do have something I want to add," Mike Watmoor, the Quality Manager says. "Doug and I had an earlier discussion about all this. I don't want to misquote you, Doug, but you seemed to be implying that we don't really have much true emphasis on our ISO documentation, meaning we see it more as a formality and not a true vehicle to guarantee effective production and quality improvement. On the other side of the coin, I don't really see this LMS system as under control, as many of you have mentioned, and really a potential risk to our Quality Management System. Speaking frankly, I am not opposed to people making suggestions and making improvements, but it simply needs to be managed better than with white boards, Post-it® Notes, and an occasional audit that always shows that no one really seems to care about how updated the boards are."

"Whoa," Jamie, the Plant Manager steps in, "We had all talked about this and really wanted to make sure we were empowering our employees and making sure we were listening to them and improving our process. We simply can't afford not to! So, when I hear you all naysaying the concept of continuous improvement, I get a little frustrated. Don't we all know we have to improve?"

"Herein lies the whole issue. Everyone in the manufacturing world knows we need to remove waste, do more with less, save money…," Tim Kech, the Finance Manager steps in. "But the real question is not whether it needs to be done, but how it should be done. I think what Doug is saying is that he is floundering. Floundering and unsure of why. He wants every employee, every valued employee, to be able to help make the process run better, cheaper, and faster. He wants to lead the charge, but as it is clearly stated by other members of the staff here, not everyone buys into the method. It's like Eliyahu Goldratt used to say: 'Many people don't really know or cannot clearly verbalize, how what they are doing is essential to the organization.' Would you be motivated if you were in that position?"

"Making suggestions at a pretty good clip is not a bad start, is it?" replies Doug, "In other words, we are creating some good energy and some decent ideas, albeit they don't all give Tim the financial numbers he is looking for right away. Maybe we should simply plod along and give it more time to become part of the culture."

"Uh, I don't think so. We realize that there are flaws in the process we have implemented. So, let's be brutally honest and simply say that we need to fix the process first, not the people," Todd, the self-proclaimed Process expert says rather boldly.

"We frequently toggle between culture and control," Janice says, "There are some of us who say that the Lean Management System needs to be driven by a true change in culture."

"Wouldn't it be leaner to simply say LMS rather than the whole three words?" Todd pipes in.

"OK, you acronymophobic!" interrupts Doug, "That's a perfect example of what we deal with around here. We want to be lean and decide to use acronyms. Then someone decides that acronyms are not good for our culture. Vicious circle again.

I think the real question is simple: Can we have both culture and control, rather than one *or* the other? I am not sure if anyone remembers this, but years ago we went through this same battle with ISO implementation. Everyone thought it was too cumbersome, a big waste of time, and totally against what we stood for as an efficient company. Come to find out, it isn't that bad, control is a positive benefit, and whether we as leaders treat it appropriately is really all that matters to its impact and effect.

I believe that our Lean implementation is weak for one single reason. We want the culture, but we don't want control. It's like wanting our kids to be happy, but not giving them any discipline. That usually results in tyranny rather than true happiness. Right? So, let's see if we can address it, not by having an either-or mindset but by having a both-are-good mindset."

There is a pause in the room.

"Well, what about my point on making sure we have the right process?" Todd asks.

"Worthy of investigation and worthy of a small pilot group to look into it," Doug responds. "Let's take that up at my next Lean meeting on Monday. Until then, I want to think about the process. As I mentioned, I am confident in what we should be doing but not so confident in how we are doing it."

Doug is now at a crossroads. He believes that *culture* must lead the initiative. He believes that control is absent. He agrees that operators get tired of new fads. He agrees that he should look at the process. But…. Can he really convince everyone of how this should work? Can he really celebrate the diversity of thought and come up with a process that agrees to everyone's suppositions? Is it like some things that need to be pushed into existence, or is it something that should be pulled? How does anyone believe that the spirit of continuous improvement should not be embedded in everything we do? All these thoughts rumble around in Doug's head as he heads off to enjoy the weekend with his family.

Actions and Discussion Points
Describe the current culture of your factory floor in 50 words or less on a separate piece of paper.
Choose one reader and have them read each description to the team, out loud and anonymously.
Reflect on each view and write 50 words or less on how that impacts your thinking.
Write 50 words or less, on a separate piece of paper, on how culture and control can coexist.
Again, have one person read each description out loud and anonymously.
Reflect on these views and write down your take-aways.

5

It's Not Always Bad to Bring Work Home with You

Doug's wife Beatrice is a real go-getter. She doesn't take no for an answer and all three of her kids are forced to live under her driven personality. Well, after the challenges and stresses at Square M's this week, Doug is simply glad to get home and find a couch to slouch into.

But at the same time, he wonders if situations at home relate to what he is trying to learn at work. As is typical for a driven spouse, the kids all have a chore list. This was originally implemented by Doug a few years ago, but it was a total flop. The writing on the dry-erase board got so dry, it was hard to scrape off, and of course, no one ended up paying attention to it. He wanted a culture in the home that was "all for one and one for all," but in reality it was more often something that simply didn't matter. Wallpaper. That was, until Beatrice took over. She has a true interest in helping her children be mature and responsible and to develop integrity. Or, simply put, 'do what you say you are going to do.' She moved the chart to an electronic screen. This was the first simple thought she had. Kids don't use dry-erase boards any more. Then, she put it on the kitchen table easel and made sure they talked about it during breakfast. It was during the chugging of orange juice and bites of cold cereal that she asked about the tasks, and most of the time, the process worked well. In fact, there is often amazing success when they all do their assignments. They get to swipe them off the screen, which is rather insignificant, but a charming sense of accomplishment.

Now, Doug thought, there is really not that much difference between the two systems. Sure, there is a component of technology thrown in there but really both systems should have worked. Both parents wanted to help their children and both loved the fact their children were actually somewhat excited about what was being done. So, how does that relate to work?

Doug decides to ask his wife about it. "So, honey, since we started doing the chore chart on the tablet, everyone has been doing a great job getting everything done. What do you think the reason for that is?" Beatrice replies rather quickly, "As you know, honey, both times we asked them to do their chores. And, we both agreed that it was important. But, when we leveraged technology with straight in-your-face leadership at the breakfast table, it really seemed to stick. Using one of *your* favorite work-isms, we had a control plan in place. As the proverb says, when we kicked off this new whole deal, 'if a man doesn't work, he doesn't eat.'"

"Yeah, the coolness, the leadership, and the control plan," Doug murmurs under his breath, "that is a very intriguing insight. I think I will consider those thoughts at our next management meeting. Honey, you've done it again. You've proved again that common sense applied anywhere is worth considering everywhere."

The meal that Beatrice prepares is especially good that night. Pad Thai noodles, broccoli, and some fried wontons.

After supper, it is time for the dishes. One rule that Doug had implemented successfully at home was that no one could eat dessert until all the pots and pans and all the meal's dishes were both cleaned and put away. Why, one might ask? Again, it was back to common sense. What better incentive than the sweet taste of homemade dessert could there be for making sure the work got done? Work before play became work before sugar. But still, Doug's mind couldn't stop trying to apply common sense. An example for how Doug's brain functioned in that regard was comparing the cycle time of the dishwasher to the length of time it would take to eat desert. Manual dishwashing and clean up, with the whole family in different roles, became a team sport and the process created a good environment to teach other life skills. The faster they worked as a team, the quicker they could eat dessert. They only needed to figure out how to deal with the "bottleneck"—the slowest part of the process. Everyone should learn how to help get the flow through the bottleneck as fast as possible. The bottleneck was the washing/rinsing process. It was one operation because the size of the workstation was simply not convenient or efficient for two people. And, Doug made sure that everyone knew this important aspect of the whole workflow.

"Make sure you don't starve the bottleneck" meant you couldn't leave dirty dishes lying around on the different counters and tables of the kitchen. You also couldn't let the dish drainer pile up, as that would be a clear example of causing the bottleneck to dawdle. That was Doug's word for causing the bottleneck to slow down or wrongly divert rather than keeping the bottleneck flowing smoothly. Doug would even say, "Go clean your hands in the bathroom! We don't have time for you to clog the bottleneck!" At times it seemed borderline schizophrenic, but Doug was convinced that this process thinking was the most efficient way to get to the dessert. Fortunately, his family was willing to learn the process and, of course, everyone did enjoy getting to the dessert as soon as possible.

This lesson in throughput was simply common sense to Doug. The goal was clear. The slowest station was clearly determined. The fastest operator, Doug, was maximizing the throughput on the station, and there were exciting incentives waiting for those who worked together as a team. Why in the world wouldn't some of his kids want to walk the 25 feet to the bathroom to wash their hands?

Herein lies the famous "common sense isn't so common" statement. When asking someone to go out of their way to serve the greater good, it can clearly be seen as an inconvenience to that person. Doug has spent a lot of time reminding his children of the real intention of the process—getting the job done as soon as possible. He reminds his daughter Abby, for the umpteenth time, "Hey, no washing your hands here at the bottleneck!" But Abby replies, "Can't I just squeeze in quickly?" Common sense from her perspective is simple. She only needs a few seconds. It isn't that big of a deal, and going over to the bathroom to wash her hands will more than triple *her* cycle time. So, when people are not seeing the goal clearly enough, common sense becomes individualistic. Abby is a sharp, fifteen year old girl with plenty of energy and frequently refers to some of her dad's favorite sayings. "Didn't you tell us once that laziness spurs efficiency?" Abby reminds her father. Doug chimes back, "Uh, more than once, my dear, but of course, your laziness in this instance is not so efficient!" Right in front of his dirty black wok, Doug has to reconsider how some sayings may spur good thoughts, but not always.

When people refer to common sense and bottleneck operations, the team has to be all on the same page. Doug may want to empower each of his children to "be all they can be" in their household duties, but clearly, he has just informed Abby that her strong drive for individual leadership and getting her hands washed is not helping the overall throughput of the process of the family getting their expected "bonus," the salted caramel and pretzel churned ice cream.

Doug reflects on this thought as he finishes up cleaning the wok and the four sets of chopsticks. Is it also true at work that the same lack of common sense for what is lean and what is removing waste is simply related to the perspective of each individual worker really trying to do the right thing when completing their individual task? Doug ponders that one for a while.

Time for ice cream.

"Dad, did you notice that we were able to sit down and enjoy this wonderful ice cream 15 seconds earlier tonight because I took the initiative to wash my hands in the bathroom?" Abby comments as they take a seat. "I thought it hadn't melted quite as much tonight," says Caleb, her older brother. "Now children," Mom steps in, "we all appreciate your ability to work together so we can now enjoy this marvelous ice cream. But, I want to ask you a question. Have you ever been to someone's house who doesn't do their dishes? Have you ever had the pleasure of contemplating the true sense of building good habits that help you learn how to work as a team, get things accomplished, and simply feel good about the condition of your kitchen?" "Mom, I know you get tired of having Dad bring work home every day, but are you talking about this 5 or 6S's stuff?" Caleb somewhat humorously asks. "Yeah, I was going to label the faucet hot and cold directionally but I figured someone might wonder if I was going overboard, since it's really not that complicated," Abby adds to the conversation. "Now, children, let's be brutally honest with each other," Doug steps up to the plate, figuratively. "I spent plenty of years living with a group of three or four other guys who simply did not have this habit or this spirit in their DNA. Pardon the acronym, but I can't pronounce the actual molecule's name. So, every night before I went to bed, I would choose to participate in serving my roommates by doing the dishes. I preferred the clean kitchen and the sense of accomplishment it gave me to help the overall functioning of the apartment. Yes, I frequently did it during times when no one was watching. But I knew that someone was watching me and that I would be rewarded someday. Maybe not with ice cream 15 seconds sooner, but with a mature character and a stronger sense of purpose."

Another opportunity to share ice cream and real life, together.

Doug and his son get up and quickly wash the few bowls and spoons, and they are all off to their own individual duties before they head off to find rest.

What has Doug learned? Lean home life is filled with simple common sense principles that need healthy leadership, incentive, and reinforcement of the benefits that come from working together. Sure, Doug knows that his kids won't always get it right away. But, building a culture takes time and leadership. Know the goal, know the slowest operation, and make sure people see the value of what you are leading them to do.

No wonder that just putting up a board with some Post-it® Notes doesn't always work.

Has Doug developed his team at work to understand that continuous improvement is difficult? Will it require training and perhaps even that challenging concept of "certification," aka ISO style, to make sure his Lean implementation is not simply a salted caramel and pretzel "flavor of the month"?

Doug 4S's his teeth, shares a few thoughts with Beatrice, and heads to find rest.

Actions and Discussion Points
How does continuous improvement create fun at your site?
What is the current benefit at your site for contributing to the continuous improvement of the site's performance?
What are the best options available to develop a more enjoyable environment at the site?
Write down how you will contribute to this environment?
Survey your employees and anonymously ask how they view their contributions to continuous improvement.

6

All for One and One for All

Doug arrives at work on Monday, realizing that his implementation of LMS up to now has been faulty. After all, he is the Lean Manager, and he really doesn't have any reason to believe that the system should fail—just like there is no reason why his kids would not be able, between their homework and electronic gaming/social networking, to get their chores done and see the common sense of how they can improve ALL processes.

So, he decides he is going to focus on the three issues that were brought to the breakfast table during his discussions at home—electronics, leadership, and control.

Doug wants first to check in with Mike, his Quality Manager, and see if he has an issue with talking about how they are going to control the LMS. "Good morning, Mike," Doug shouts as he walks into the Quality Assurance lab where Mike is reviewing an inspection report from Bilher #1 and all the problems it experienced last week. "Hey, Doug, how was your weekend?" Mike asks, "I was hoping you would come in and blast me with some visionary statement about controlling your LMS."

"Well, Janice was very thankful that I allowed the Bilher #1 operator to shut down the machine on his own authority, and sure enough, he and Mike got the tooling back into proper position, so we were able to meet your customer-honoring Cpk requirements! How's that for a good start?" Doug replied.

"I have been looking at the numbers, and quite honestly, I'm impressed. Even though we ran all weekend, we had no quality issues, and Bilher #4 is clearly in shape this week to not be starved for parts and cause us to miss customer delivery dates. Nice work for an empowerment guru," Mike says half-jokingly.

"Really, Mike, I have thought long and hard about what you said, and quite frankly, I came to the conclusion … that I agree with you."

There is a long pause.

Doug wonders if Mike actually heard what he said or was too occupied with his reflections on Bilher #1 data that it simply went over his head.

"Sorry for the late reply," Mike finally notes, "but, quite honestly, I am shocked and pleasantly surprised. Not that

I actually know the perfect solution but at least we are starting to be on the same page."

"Mike, let me ask you a question. In all your 43 years of manufacturing experience, have you ever seen a production process that is … hindered by a clear training document?" Doug purposely pauses there for effect. "Well, to be frank with you, Doug, I have lived in both worlds where people aren't given a standard, and where they are provided a clear description of the task we ask them to do to a certain standard. The impact is significantly better when we have a standard. I have no doubt about that," Mike responds. "However, the other issue I have relates to what I consider the 'secret sauce' of success." Doug turns his head slightly and says, "which is ….?" Mike continues, "We need to always find a qualified certified trainer. This is unquestionably the most important aspect of the entire process of training. If you don't have a good trainer, the trainee will not be trained. Sorry to use common sense, but that is simply what always needs to be done."

"So, what you are telling me is that there are two critical aspects to the process. One is a sound training document, and another is a sound trainer? *Sounds* like a reasonably easy process to implement, right?" Doug asks. Mike, with his four decades of experience, gently responds, yes, it is 'easy' as you say, if and only if, you have people in the organization who are ready to understand the process and are qualified to properly train their colleagues. When it comes to Bilher #1, that was pretty easy. Jay does an excellent job helping people understand how to run the machine, and as we just noticed last weekend, does an even better job of setting a good example of working together with his team to make sure we get the machine up and running as soon as possible. The guy is a huge benefit to our organization and is unbelievably humble at the same time. A great trainer for a critical machine is certainly what we have been blessed with.

"That being said, I think we have an issue when it comes to throwing another, and I mean 'another' management system, into the mix without proper understanding of the process, without a clear training document on how to do the job, and without making sure we have a certified trainer to make sure people can effectively lead an improvement meeting." Mike takes a deep breath and professionally and politely states, "Do you know how hard it is to lead a group of independent, diverse, talented employees? Are you actually thinking that you could just put up some boards with different columns, assign a leader, and create an environment where improvement happens? Now, I get the fact that some people out there might be naturally good at taking on that kind of new responsibility, but quite frankly, I think it is an error on our part not to make sure, when we give someone a new role, that we properly train and certify them to perform the task at hand. I know some groups are awesome, but some have people that love to take entire meetings off course with their own individual gripes and opinions. Leading that type of person or that type of meeting would certainly take some training and development."

Doug also takes a deep breath.

"I am so glad we are on the same page, Mike. It reminds me of a recent meeting that went well off course when someone wanted to argue how many S's there are in a 5S event! Some of our people excel at what they are naturally gifted at doing, while many others are simply floundering in their assigned role. At the factory floor level, we make the product that customers buy. We can't really consider empowering employees to improve the processes without developing their skills first. And, if you want me to add a little fuel to the fire, how about we discuss the next role of management, the role of making sure our factory floor improvement meetings are successfully supported with resources or clear, respectful communication on ideas that might need a 'no' or 'not now' answer?

"Can we work on a training and certification document for our teams together?" Doug asks his long-time colleague and controlled document friend.

"Why, sure. From my perspective, blending the Quality Management System with the newly introduced Lean Management System is what we as a leadership team clearly need to accomplish for our teams and for the sake of our esteemed customers."

"I'll start putting pen to paper right away. There's nothing like feeling empowered to change and improve things with a guy committed to making sure we keep working stable and to a standard. Maybe we can start a sitcom 'The Odd Couple,'" Doug humorously comments as he heads to his office with a new-found passion to lead by example and work together. The thought crosses Doug's mind, "I wonder if Mike likes salted caramel and pretzel churned ice cream?"

Actions and Discussion Points
How does continuous improvement define the required training at your site today?
How does the Quality department view controlling the training and certification of the process?
How does a certified trainer get chosen for roles at this site?
How would you choose a continuous improvement meeting leader?

7

Friends at Last

Lean thinking can be difficult. There is nothing more humbling than to realize that the quest to improve manufacturing processes with an empowered workforce is a difficult job. Doing Lean is different than becoming Lean. Counting the number of Kaizen events can be different than developing a team of people committed to improving the processes in everyday life. Doug

isn't attempting to renounce how "short events of people committed to addressing issues and improving a process" can make great gains in productivity, but he is more interested in creating a trained army of leaders that know how to create a culture of continuous improvement.

Doug spends a few weeks and comes up with the following standard. It is different than most of the historical ISO training documents. Mike admits that normal Manager staff meetings don't usually get put under document control. Lean people like to talk about Leader Standard Work, but rarely do they want to commit to being audited. Doug brings a rough draft for Mike to look at. "So, this document talks about things that relate to running and leading a meeting—purpose, expected outcomes, even ideal behaviors. Isn't that interesting?" "Yes, I am not sure how the ISO community will understand it all, but let's take a look."

ISO-Controlled Document

SQM-LMS-T-001   **09/24/20xx**

Tier One Shift Meeting Leader Standard Work

The ISO controlled document should accomplish the following in our Tier One Leader Standard Work:

In an environment committed to safety, the efficient end-of-shift meeting should clarify:

1. After clear communication at the start of the shift, did we succeed to meet today's objective as a team?
2. What can we do to improve or learn?
3. Are we setting up the next shift for success?

It should explain clearly:

A. Purpose of the meeting
B. Expected outcomes of the meeting
C. Ideal behaviors for the meeting attendees and meeting leader
D. Visual communication process requirements
   Keep it simple—easy to read and understand—not too busy or complex
   Easy to see who owns what on the board
   Easy to see any timing and/or priority

Easy to see improvement process going on

Easy to see support is being demonstrated

E. Additional information—templates, best practices, FAQs

F. It should have a training sign-off and a certification sign-off by a certified trainer and the trainee to verify that both agree the training has been completed and was successful. An example follows:

I have been trained to this standard, meaning it has been clearly explained to me how meetings should be led to help our teams know if they are winning, if they are learning, and if we are continually solving problems and improving.

_____		_____	
Employee	Date	Trainer	Date

I have been certified to this standard, meaning I have led the meetings and have demonstrated the behaviors that show I know its content and support the intention and purpose of our organization to be safe, to be winning, improving, and learning through Tier One meetings.

_____		_____	
Employee	Date	Trainer	Date

"Well, what do you think?" Doug asks Mike, "Does it fit the first aspect of the requirement you gave me, that it clearly communicates what is required of the job as improvement meeting leader?" Mike, being an experienced Quality Manager with many years of experience reviewing documents, quickly looks through the document and says, "Well, at first blush... it is rather unique. That being said … I like it. We can certainly embellish the sections so everyone understands things like ideal behaviors, but this is a great place to start."

Whoa, Doug thought to himself, now we are getting somewhere. "Why don't you think on it for a while, and I will set up a meeting early next week to discuss it. That will give you time to contemplate its worth to our organization. As you might guess, the other aspect of the standard is also clearly on my mind."

"Yep, mine too." Mike says rather quietly, "I hope we can find the right certified trainer."

Actions and Discussion Points
Who should be a part of the initiative to create a training document?
Review the different sections offered in the book for the training document. Which would you include, add, or delete?
How involved should different levels of the organization be in this creation of the standard?
Will any outside benchmarking or feedback be used? Why or why not?
Write your personal reflections on the current state of the process.

8

Keeping Things Rolling

Next week comes rolling in with its typical barrage of manufacturing emergencies and a plethora of meetings, all crying out for attention and action items. Doug muses, "If only we had a more engaged and empowered workforce to get all this stuff figured out."

As promised, Doug had set up the meeting with Mike, the Quality Manager, to review the controlled document for training Tier One meeting leaders.

But to Doug's surprise, the meeting ends up including more than just quality. Mike has brought along a General Supervisor on the floor named Dave, as well as the Manufacturing Manager Lori, and the Internal Auditor, Sheryl. Despite Doug not having been informed of these changes to the meeting, the additional attendees provide him a sense of confidence for a better discussion and potential buy-in.

Doug kicks off with, "Well, I assume all of you had a chance to look at the proposed standard for helping our valued employees understand their important role in leading continuous improvement meetings." "Yes, we have all read it, but that doesn't mean we all think it's a good idea, right?!" Lori pipes in. "You really think we can get this to work and run the Lean Management System without any findings? Are you crazy? You know how it's going out there, don't you?" Dave adds, "The boards are usually dilapidated, out of date, or simply not very impressive, to say the least."

A rather long moment of silence occurs. Then Doug responds.

"Honestly, have we led this initiative successfully? I don't think so, and I'll take the blame. We had an excellent corporate system roll-out with promises of a brighter future, but I didn't do my due diligence. We had the nerve to roll out an 'additional' management system, which by the way doesn't sound very lean to me, with assigned duties and responsibilities without any training and certifying of this extremely important job! This would cause almost any new job to fail. Wouldn't it? Didn't we all subscribe to the importance of making sure our employees are sufficiently trained to do their jobs? Are we out of our minds to think that all our continuous improvement meeting leaders would simply, by osmosis, pick up the skills to drive a challenging manufacturing environment toward improved productivity? If I pause and think about that for a minute, I must simply say 'No way!' So, as a solution, I am suggesting that we blend the two management systems together. We document our new job, we document that we trained the person to do the job, and we document the fact that they feel confident to do the job and consider themselves certified to do the job. Why would we not consider this common sense?"

Doug takes a purposeful, important pause, and then continues.

"We need to change the culture here so that every worker is part of the network of empowered problem solvers. Easy to say, but very difficult to deliver on. Sure, we would all love that to be the case, but have we as leaders agreed to develop, support, and provide resources for our people to do this?

I know that many of us cringe at the thought of adding another document into our burgeoning collection of controlled documents, but how else can we verify sustainability to the system? How can we guarantee that we haven't left our continuous improvement meeting leaders without sufficient training and resources to do the job we ask of them? How can we call ourselves leaders of this culture change, when all we really want to do is post something on boards, cover our tracks for our own continuous improvement meetings, and then go to the floor and talk in a foreign language, when people simply want to be heard, be respected, and be part of improving our processes? Don't we get it?" Doug again stops for a reflective moment.

"Any questions?" Doug asks, expecting a rather hostile response.

"Mike, what are your thoughts on it?" Lori asks. "Well, after reviewing it this weekend and having a great deal of respect for Doug's intentions, I cannot state it would completely address the process. The training document is unique enough, but the other thing I have a concern about is whether we will have a qualified certified trainer to ensure all of our continuous improvement meeting leaders are properly and successfully trained." "Yes," Dave steps in, "I really appreciate the intention, and I see there are some good descriptions of ideal behaviors that should be taking place in the meetings, but I find it a little difficult to think we could actually get ideal behavior." "Yes," Doug notes, "and that is exactly why we use the term 'ideal.' We don't expect this will happen often, but we do want people to know the types of behaviors we expect in a meeting. In time, if we were to run the gamut on this standard, as would be common sense, we would also help the attendees of the meeting know what the standard is. Part of the strategy would be to schedule group meetings to go over this and have the attendees sign off on having seen and agreed to the intention of the meetings. Of course, I want to make sure the improvement meeting leaders get properly trained before we go to others."

"You know, I am warming up to the idea," Lori cautiously adds. "We have to lead the culture. We have to make sure we have sufficiently developed our people to do their job. But, how do we make sure that the upper tiers of this improvement process support the factory floor meetings?"

"So glad you asked," Doug responds, "My suggestion is to 'use common sense'. We provide a spot on the board for the leader to indicate whether or not they need support from the upper tiers. That way, we have a form of accountability, assuming the Plant Manager Jamie will enforce it, to make sure we are supporting people in being successful. That would be a real paradigm shift to the pyramid of life, wouldn't it? And if, we are picking good leaders for the meetings and making sure they are well trained, this will only bring more confidence to the satisfaction metric."

"So, it really boils down to our leadership commitment to create this improvement process within our ISO-controlled documentation system of ISO 9001:2015, which clearly already has a section on requiring us to have some sort of process of on-going improvement," Mike declares. "If this really works like it is supposed to, we should be back to one Quality Management System, which will make us accountable for supporting the improvement ideas provided by our employees at all levels. How could a Quality Manager not be satisfied with that?!"

"Yeah, and since we have a poorly-working layered process audit built into the current Lean Management System, why don't we shift it to a layered process coaching of the value of each section of our ISO system?" says Sheryl. "That way we would be using the LMS system to reinforce and help everyone adhere to the agreed upon ISO system. That would be like a match made in manufacturing heaven!"

"Great idea, Sheryl!" Doug mentions. "This is exactly the teamwork we are looking for!"

"On top of all that, I have another idea that might further develop the tender balance between standardization and unstable experimentation and change. Are you ready for this?" Doug questions the small crowd. Everyone, understanding that silence is consent, agrees.

"OK, remember what you told me about what happened last weekend with your old Buick LeSabre, Dave?" Doug asks. "Yeah, I wanted to make sure I knew the best way to quickly change the oil, so I didn't have to spend so much money at the shop. I searched on YouTube and, boom, there it was. You know me, always trying to be frugal."

"Yes, that is the normal way almost everyone learns how to do an operation these days. There are whole sites committed to helping people know how to fix stuff, not to mention simply searching YouTube to see what all you can learn about your make and model," Doug mentions. "We have always heard that a picture is worth a thousand words, but then how much is a video worth?" Well, at 30 frames per second, a one minute video would be worth about 1.8 million words. So, mathematically, that would be a 7,200 page written Operating procedure. That just doesn't feel right! Dave quips. "I didn't even know math had feelings," Lori chimes in. "So, regardless of the data analytics going on, I think we can all agree that we can also move our training into the next generation and make sure that we make it usable and beneficial for the employees," Doug says, "In fact, putting a QR code on the machines or the boards would allow people to easily access the training documents. I know this might frighten some of us, but if we could conveniently access our documents, we might actually use them more effectively, and better yet, we could attach suggestions for improving the actual Standards directly online. Whoa, wouldn't that be shocking?!"

"We already have access to software with a very user-friendly interface where we could not only upload video, but also add arrows, color coding, and even load in improvement videos for all the other shifts to view and give comment on," Doug said. "Does that mean we could film an excellent example of a continuous improvement meeting?" Dave asks. "Of course." Doug responds, "We already have some instruction videos on the suggested controlled document. We could certainly add a few good meeting examples."

"OK," Mike concludes, "so we are all in on leading this charge ..., together?"

"Not so fast," Doug interrupts, "Who is going to be our certified trainer?" Doug is very impressed that he stuck that question back into the conversation.

"I'm sorry, but I think we need to use that old buzzword or whatever they call it—common sense—again," Lori speaks up, implying her enthusiasm is growing stronger. "Why don't we get together as a team and find out if we have any superstars out there that we can certify and use to train their colleagues? If we don't, we could come up with a plan to get interested people to join in the work." Dave adds, having an inside scoop on Doug's favorite dessert, "Yeah, consider offering some incentive, maybe even some salted caramel and pretzel ice cream, to get some buy-in and get this done right. From my experience, if we pick the right people, we will get the best solution."

"I love it when we work together," Doug responds. "Let me try to summarize what we are attempting to accomplish; I'll write it on the white board here:

1. We don't want an additional management system (LMS) that is flying solo without effective standard controls, proper training, solid certified leaders, and a clear way for the factory continuous improvement leaders to visually and verbally communicate that they are satisfied with leadership support.
2. As leaders, we want to hold ourselves responsible for selecting, training, and certifying our continuous improvement leaders on the floor and then make sure we support their success in leading our more and more engaged workforce.
3. We want to make sure our training documentation takes on a more useful role in improving the quality of our service and processes for the sake of our customers. Part of this improvement involves the utilization of leveraging our standards digitally to attach improvement ideas and suggestions.
4. We want to utilize the layered process audit of the LMS system to coach others on the value of the ISO system.

5. We realize that changing a culture takes time, leadership, implementation of sensible technology, and a growing appreciation for the value of our employees.

6. We agree to minimize acronyms and buzzwords, keeping our words in our native language. So, no Gemba walking. We can easily go out to the floor, which is the real place.

Does that sound like a good plan?" Doug calls out.

The silence is golden. Heads are nodding. Doug is content with the plan. He realizes that life doesn't just flow from a plan. It flows through leadership, persistence, selecting the right people, and having a solid, clearly communicated strategy.

After a long pause, Doug breaks the silence, "OK, I will carry the plan forward to Jamie and the other managers, and you will be invited to the continuous improvement 'improvement' meeting. Meeting adjourned."

Actions and Discussion Points
Write down in your own words how your site would be able to make a commitment to the continuous improvement strategy within the ISO Quality Management System.
Discuss how to include video enhancement into your development of the system.
Many programs and initiatives stall and become nonsustainable. ISO is one way to maintain the sustainability. What else will be needed?

9

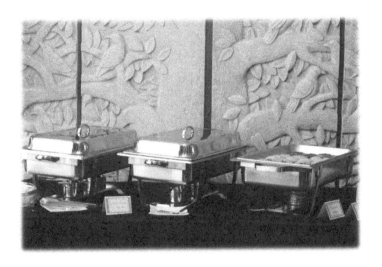

Letting off Some Steam

After a relatively successful meeting, Doug finds time to head out to the floor with some renewed enthusiasm for the improvement process he envisions and how it will actually value the employees' inputs and efforts. And guess who he sees first? None other than Ron Schechter, the incredibly strongly-opinioned Union Steward who always feels the need to explain why every single management decision is meant to screw the employees over. He constantly looks for reasons to spread the seeds of doubt and confusion among his Union colleagues. Doug finds this a little frustrating but always works to consider Ron's input and extract anything positive. He makes sure that Ron sees the benefit of the organization's plan to improve the processes.

"So, Ron, how's it going?" Doug asks as he stops by Bilher #3 to have a brief visit. "Oh, not so good," Ron snipes back, hoping to get a rise out of Doug, but to no avail. "I've been wondering when you are actually going to help us be more successful with our production numbers. It seems we waste more time sharing good ideas with people that don't care than we do actually fixing things. All I can see with all these boards is a bunch of bleeding red markers with no real intention to make things better? I'm tired of hearing that we're supposed to 'embrace the red.' How about we actually listen and fix the issues so we don't have to embrace so much?"

Doug, cautious with his words, responds, "Thanks for the input, Ron. I know I can always count on you for providing feedback. As a matter of fact, we are working on improving the improvement process, which I know you have been an avid communicator of." Note Doug does not use the word 'supporter.' "I think Bilher #3 has had a good run of productivity, never shutting down the bottleneck recently, and I am very appreciative for that." Ron, a rather arrogant fellow, gives his typical response, "Yeah, it's about time you noticed. But then again, you are often noticing little issues that don't really help my bonus much. They might look pretty on the board, but I am not sure they are putting anything in my wallet, eh?!"

Doug challenges Ron's response, "So, can you think of anything you have suggested that we aren't working on?" A long pause. Sometimes Ron's bark is worse than his bite. More pause. So, Doug follows up, "Well, if you do, let me know. I respect the insights you gather from others, and I want to make sure I learn from them." While this maybe wasn't a perfect discussion, Doug feels like allowing Ron to let off some steam is always a good idea.

Doug wanders back to the tool room where he finds time to discuss how life is treating Mike Tharms. Mike is an awesome toolmaker, but is said to be not too interested in supporting production. He simply wants to be left alone and be allowed to do whatever the work orders say he should do. Doug, knowing how talented Mike is, thinks otherwise. "Hey, Mike, how was your weekend?" "Not bad. Got a chance to catch some bass." They go on to discuss the typical details surrounding the whole fishing experience with each other, and then Doug starts the transition. "Sounds good. Hey, by the way, did you get a chance to build any of those spare jaw packages for the AMI Dial machines? We thought if we always had a spare on deck out there, it would make it easier for you to simply fix up the broken one after we reinstalled the spare one." "Yeah, I have about 1/2 of them completed. Your idea made a lot of sense to me, so I've been working on it when I have time." Doug was impressed. "Whoa, thanks. Seems like we have a good shot of getting our OEE up over 92 percent with work like you're doing. Thanks." "Yeah, no problem." Oops! A dreaded acronym creeps up again. This OEE metric is uptime of making good product. With a 24-station dial assembly machine with eight vibratory bowl machines and a manual load station, this is a pretty impressive result.

Doug once again sees how willing people are to do things that make "common sense." Mike Harms is a great toolmaker but he has also been helping with downtime on the bottleneck. With 24 stations on the dial, it's easy to have one go haywire, and Mike's work is well worth its weight in gold. When Doug was Supervisor, back in the day, he taught everyone on 3rd shift the "3 bucks, 3 bucks, 3 bucks" slogan. That was how much money was made every second the machine ran. While the number wasn't exactly right, it served the purpose of getting people to understand the real impact on the bottleneck operation. Quite a blessing to have the "you'll never get that guy to help" guy helping out.

Next Doug takes a walk out to the AMI machines. And guess what, the analog machines are actually creating some disruptions, and who else is helping unload the AMI machine to make sure it keeps running and doesn't dawdle, but Todd, the maintenance guy! Now, that is a real treat. Normally, the kind of guy you don't see too much, he is actually unloading boxes of breakers to make sure there is no stopping at the AMI bottleneck. And, he is also putting them back on when the analogs start moving again. Doug is rather astonished. Of course, he keeps in mind that one of the most attractive female workers is at the station where Todd is helping, but regardless, Doug truly appreciates the effort. "Nice work, Todd. Thanks for adding to your bonus." Todd nods and continues to talk to Barb.

Progress is slow, but encouraging…. Time to head home and see what is happening on the home front.

Actions and Discussion Points
Discuss the importance of walking the floor during the original introduction of the process. Write down your view.
Describe, in your own words, the importance of walking the floor as a normal practice of leading effective manufacturing improvement.
Discuss the process that will be put into place to make sure this becomes the actual behavior of the leaders.
Discuss how to reduce the number of meetings to have more time to walk the floor and support the employees.
Set a deadline to remove two meetings from your monthly schedule.

10

Getting Total Leadership Buy-in

The process of getting everyone at home on the same page is challenging, even if Doug is simply attempting to get all the dishes done. Often life in general is filled with a matrix of opportunities and support systems that call for strong leadership, good understanding, and a form of character development that works something like what an old Jewish king once said, "Haughtiness goes before destruction; humility *precedes* honor." Doug wants to share what he's learning at work, but decides that it is better to focus on the issues at hand. "How's it going, Caleb?" Caleb, looking up from his electronic gaming experience, mumbles, "Oh, OK." "Isn't your college common application deadline today?" Doug calmly mentions. "Yes, I'll get to it in just a little bit."

Doug sees the daily grind of developing character and leading people at work to be much the same as at home. He has several options to reply. Get mad. Keep silent. Don't do anything. Start an argument. Call in additional resources (his wife). Celebrate and show interest in Caleb's performance on the electronic game. How one leads a discussion, especially when it is not heading in the right direction, is a very important aspect of success. Doug has, after plenty of haughty moments, learned quite a bit about directing his children. And sure enough, before the night is over, Caleb has successfully completed his application, on time, and has graciously received his parents' "improvement" suggestions.

Work is much the same way. We can find the exceptional person who simply is a genius when it comes to inspiring, listening, leading, directing, and redirecting conversation to create a great environment of teamwork and improvement results. Doug mentions some of what he's learned to his wife, "You know, dear, I sure have made a lot of mistakes when it comes to helping our children improve and be all they can be." Her response is simple, "Yeah, I know." Enough said. With that in mind, and with the spirit of humility, they decide to find rest for the night.

The breakfast of champions—a combination of half a bottle of yesterday's diet cola and two granola bars—sets Doug in motion to start a very important day. As he drives to the plant, he knows he needs to accomplish a very significant benchmark today. He is contemplating that thought when he enters the plant and meets the quiet but friendly security guard, Bob, at the door. "Morning, Bob." "Morning, Doug." "Anything new and exciting happen last night on your duty?" "Nope." Doug knows that even though one would rarely consider Bob an extrovert, he always seems to know what is going on in the plant. He is a great addition to the process of managing safety and security at the plant, and Doug lets him know, "Thanks again for your watchful eye and friendly welcome to my day." "No problem," Bob replied, "Have a good day." Doug remembers the amazing insight Bob has always had when things "happen" at the plant and realizes once more, how important every individual is to the factory's success.

After settling into his office with a cup of coffee, Doug quickly prepares for the day.

Caffeine helps some, but there's nothing like an early morning meeting to get the blood boiling. Especially when it relates to having the privilege to perform the amazing feat of getting all the leadership on the same page when it comes to implementation of a successful Lean culture. Doug knows Jamie, the Plant Manager, is all about numbers. Janice usually deals with whatever fires happen to be going on for the day, and the other manufacturing managers, other than newly converted Lori, are lukewarm to the whole Lean process and improvement meetings that, in their area, don't really happen consistently. Sure, there are boards with some occasional information relevant to the current week, but usually they consist of old news that no one looks at or cares about. Doug knows he has his work cut out for him.

"Good morning, everyone," Jamie kicks off the meeting at 8:02 a.m., "Nice to see everyone here for a very important discussion. But before we discuss anything, I want to share with you the monthly results we just received from Tim last night. I don't want to put this too drastically, but we didn't do well at all. As you know, we did have a few service interruptions that exasperated the problem, but it appears that our competition is eating us for lunch. Now, I realize that we've already gone through one workforce reduction in the last 12 months, but we really need everyone to be fully on board to drive significant improvement in our results. I know all of us are aware of our various red indicators, and I think the people on the floor are also aware. Our turns are too low, our quality continues to suffer, and I certainly don't feel a very strong spirit of continuous improvement out there. I know I haven't had much time for Gemba walks, but the few times I am out there, I don't see much vim and vigor."

A rather painful, long quiet pause fills the room with an air of fear.

Jamie has been known to overreact to certain metrics and numbers, so this is not entirely unusual, but it is still always difficult to deal with. Doug knows that having an excellent culture of working together as a team is not only great for the results, but it also creates a fantastic work environment. He yearns to make it a reality and get everyone out of this funk as soon as possible, but he also knows that his strategy requires complete leadership commitment and a clear acceptance of the strategy.

Each member of the management team takes time to share an update from their side of the business. Jamie remains calm, but no one really feels too excited about sharing their results. Of course, Todd, the self-proclaimed process genius, throws in his typical engineering slant on how everyone else screws up his machines, but the rest of the crowd is used to that and simply lets it slide by. Engineering can be easier to manage, as its metrics are not so easy to measure, unlike things such as cost of goods sold, and that always provides Todd with a little more freedom.

Last, but certainly not least, on the agenda is the Lean Manager, Doug. Sometimes he feels like he has "doug" himself into a deep pit, where Kaizens done and number of improvement ideas submitted simply don't cut the mustard. But, Doug knows he has a few supporters in the crowd, so he takes a swing and begins to make his pitch for improving the improvement process.

"Today is a rather special day. One that I hope you all remember for the rest of your manufacturing lives."

A long, deafening pause follows.

"And, to get it all started," Doug installs yet another dramatic pause, "I have prepared a special breakfast snack for you." The crowd, generally used to having the typical snacks for meetings, prepares for coffee and perhaps some Danish rolls. But, Doug proceeds to pull over the stadium-style cooler from under the table. Janice comments first, "Did someone suggest on a Post-it® Note that the leaders get more 'cultured' with yogurt, pardon the pun?" "No, something better than breakfast yogurt," Doug responds, "We get ... salted caramel and pretzel churned ice cream!" Whoa. The crowd is a little stunned, especially given the two overriding flavors in the room—bad results and early morning!

"Let me try to explain," Doug begins his important paradigm-shifting soliloquy. "When we think of the factory and its ability to be successful during constant cost and competitive pressures, the normal default idea that frequently gets discussed is, 'How are we leveraging our entire workforce to get the results we need?' Jamie, I think you have mentioned this even as recently as this morning. After a rather dismal start to our Lean Manufacturing System roll out, I think it's time we stop, have some ice cream, and discuss a new paradigm that is filled with more common sense. So, with that as a prelude to my upcoming soapbox speech, let's have some ice cream." Doug starts dishing out the soft ice cream, hopefully making the statement: We should always look at things from a new angle. Ice cream isn't usually served for breakfast, right? After serving everyone, Doug gives his clear point of view, with the goal of getting everyone on the same page, "You know, I have been part of the Lean movement within manufacturing for a little more than 27 years. For those of you that are doing the math, this means that I started in manufacturing quite a while ago. I only recently have been in the particular function of 'Lean.' I have been an Industrial Engineer, a Material Control Manager, a Plant Operations Manager, a Third-Shift Supervisor, a Senior Supervisor leading other Supervisors, a Cost Engineer, a Materials Manager, a Purchasing Manager, an Oversees Purchasing Specialist, a Supply Chain Director, and a VP of Supply Chain. I have opened and managed an ISO-13485 site in China, worked for more than a decade in a Union environment, and have had the pleasure of walking an employee out the door after more than 100 pages of documentation regarding their inappropriate behavior. I have created a successful succession plan for my Operations Manager's role and have spent two different stints working with some rather unimpressive consulting firms to help drive projects that reduce cost of goods sold. I've been an ISO internal auditor and have supervised every department in a manufacturing facility. Without trying to create the impression that I have been there and have done that, I do have a historical perspective on how Lean developed in manufacturing. Quite honestly, I have been disappointed with the types of initiatives that came out of Lean programs within the previous firms that I have worked for. The Lean departments tend to be islands unto themselves, with much less experience out in the real world of manufacturing than they should have, and large sets of 'tools' that they think are easy to employ to remove waste. They generally have a friendly attitude toward employees and realize that there are plenty of opportunities to go after in a manufacturing site. Sure, if there is a good leader with some good understanding of manufacturing, there will be good results. But, many times, this hasn't been the case from my experience, and the metrics that they tout are generally about the softer side of driving effective productivity.

Let me put it another way. A Lean leader can be seen as an 'add-on' to help drive the culture of continuous improvement, but they are clearly not the ones with the positional authority to manage all aspects of the culture. In other words, they are individual contributors.

Now, we all know that within this committee of leaders who have just finished their first servings of churned ice cream for breakfast, we all play a part in driving a culture that is non-yogurt-based. We want everyone engaged and empowered, but at the same time we don't really have any clear strategy for getting that done within our own teams, because it is the Lean Manager's job to do that. We also know that if we did have everyone on the same page and participating in improving our processes, surely, Jamie would fully support that." Doug leans over and recognizes the most important person in the room.

"Well, here is my strategy. It comes with a proven track record, and it comes with the full support of our very seasoned Quality Manager." Doug leans over to give strong recognition to Mike.

"When we were asked to roll out this corporate Lean strategy, we willingly jumped in with both feet, put up boards with specific columns, and even followed the standard for the width of the lines that separated the individual columns. We did see value in the standardization of all of Square M's facilities, and so we followed along carefully and methodically. But, in conversations across our entire organization, including many of the other sites, I have been given the same general feedback…. It's not going too well.

Doug continues, Thinking outside the ice box," referring to the unique dessert, "let's attempt to use an analogy that will hopefully resonate with all of you. Let's all remember back to when we implemented our automated assembly line here at our site. It was an awesome set of machines and an awesome display of engineering genius." Doug leans over to give a nod to Todd, but without saying his name, since Todd already has a reasonably high level of self-confidence.

"We didn't exactly have a smooth start up, but that was to be expected. We were attempting a very difficult project, namely getting one machine to do what more than 50 people used to do by hand. Did we think that we could simply drop this machine onto the floor, put a newly assigned automation technician in front of it, and hope it went well?" Doug, as usual, allows a healthy pause to fall on the room, but not long enough to allow anyone to step in and ruin the flow of his thoughts. "We had the company that built the machine out on the floor, working constantly with Jay to make sure everyone knew how the machine worked and how to get it running and how to adjust it and how to clean it and how to …. Get my point? We accepted it for what it was—a new job that required plenty of coaching and development and confirmation that we had a person—Jay—who could run the job well.

As you know, we developed a training and certification process for the job and had Jay sign off on it, just like we would any other job we have in this whole factory. There was no debating any of the decisions we made. We documented that Jay was trained and certified and made sure he had plenty of coaching to guarantee he could do the job well.

Well you all know that life isn't perfect. We could all easily drone on about how the machine was down last week for a considerable length of time and we still must be learning how to make efficient use of all our resources in the facility.

It's a never-ending process of ... on-going continuous improvement.

But my point is clear—to make sure we have a solid management system in place, we have to train and certify the people that we ask to do the job. Is everyone following me so far?" Doug pauses for a check on the crowd, who are probably still wondering what the real point is. And sure enough, Janice says, "OK, thanks for reminding us of the history and the headaches we're currently experiencing over the Bilher #1 uptime, but what point are you really trying to make? Or does that come after our second helping of caramel and pretzels?"

Doug leads off again, "So glad you asked, Janice. I want to discuss what I consider to be that same common sense we used when we rolled out the new equipment and what we had to do and apply it to the *monumental* task of changing our culture here. There isn't one of us in this room who doesn't know that we are the ones responsible for the culture here. We as leaders set the tone, decide on the strategy and the processes we want to use, and then must manage these things to create the great results we all long and work 60-hour weeks for.

So, here it is in plain, straightforward language. We implemented an entirely new *additional* management system that is completely outside of our strategic and preferred ISO controlled document process, put up some boards with crystal clear lines and columns, and asked our teams on the factory floor to change our culture. No training like Jay got, no documentation to verify that the people we asked to do that job felt trained and certified, and no daily coaching by the machine/system designer.

Is it any wonder we aren't doing so well?" Doug stops, leans towards Todd, the rather confident Engineering Manager, and says pointedly, "The last time I checked the CAD files, I was thoroughly blown away by the complexity of the human brain and all the unique systems components, such as ears, tongues, eyes, and noses that work in conjunction with that unbelievably well-designed cranium system. Why, it can work so well with the nose that it can smell hypocrisy and lack of commitment a mile away.... If we asked Tier leaders to run a continuous improvement meeting every day, which by the way, *relies* on upper tier support, and didn't provide them the proper resources to get that job done, I think we would be considered out of our 'common sense' mind!

The process of creating a culture requires a commitment to support and develop the culture. Hence, the first critical statement: 'We need to control this process under ISO.' While many of us may have never thought of it, I would simply suggest handing Jay a new automated yoke assembly machine and asking him why he is failing to get it to run smoothly. If we really want to secure our futures and commit to creating a continuous improvement culture, we need to, like with any other process out on the floor, bring it into our already existing, already auditable management system."

Mike, uncharacteristically, lets out a hearty, "Amen!"

Doug continues, "We need this process of ongoing improvement, to be trained, certified, and auditable. Yes, that means we might have a 'finding' and get into trouble with our dear ISO auditing teams, but so be it. Why not be accountable to do what we said we would do? Aren't we supposed to lead with a high level of integrity and transparency?

And while I am on the subject, we must also address the difference between just checking a box on a form and selecting the right people to do the job—leading continuous improvement meetings out on the floor. Maybe some of you were born yesterday, but this simply isn't an easy job to do. Have you ever tried to have a healthy discussion with Ron and felt like you were really making progress? So, to add to the ISO controlled documentation, we need, like any other job in this plant, to have a clearly organized and systematic way to be chosen for leading continuous improvement meetings. Perhaps it would include incentive pay or other logical enhancements to demonstrate that it is an important job? I have been absolutely impressed with the caliber of people and processes we put in place to make sure we were running our new automated equipment the right way. We need to follow the same strategy for the job of leading a group of highly complex and utterly important employees to develop our processes.

Finally, when we purchased the new machines, we brought very qualified employees from the machine design department and allowed them 6 months to assist our teams in making sure the process ran well. In continuous improvement meeting speak that means we must also selectively appoint certified trainers to the task of coaching our continuous improvement meeting leaders. This job is tough and requires a very broad skill set that not many people have. As a leadership team, we need to dwell on that, and make sure we have the right people in place for that.

So, in conclusion and before I hand over the podium, we need to commit to 4 things:

1. We need to look at our organization and develop our continuous improvement process, develop standards and training, and load it into our ISO documentation.
2. We need to select certified trainers in each of our departments that will successfully commit time to develop our continuous improvement meeting leaders.
3. We need to work with our certified trainers to make sure we effectively select the right improvement meeting leaders.
4. We need to walk through a clear process with our factory employees, so they can understand why we are doing what we are doing and how we will manage the change.

As you might have heard, I have already created much of this documentation. I am ready to start this caramel and pretzel strategy as soon as we can all, as leaders, realize how significant this culture change is to our organization. Each of us must lead our teams with passionate support for our employees in making this an exciting ongoing improvement environment.

So …. Who wants a second helping of ice cream? Who's in?"

After a reasonable amount of "deafening silence," Doug breaks it up. "Apart from the enthusiasm of creating this culture change, I want to also introduce better documentation for our training. Here's my final point:

5. We need to leverage video, like we all do on the weekends when we want to know how to do stuff. Training manuals are great, and one-on-one personal training is even better, but we think it would be good to have our Subject Matter Experts load their 30+ years of manufacturing wisdom to a medium that is 1.8 million times better than the written word. Remember, a picture's worth a thousand words. For you engineers and mathematicians in the room, that is 60 second video, at 30 frames per second, times 1,000 words per picture. Additionally, we could stop making suggestions with Post-it® Notes that are hard to read, and instead provide a video that clearly communicates the improved way of doing something. I do get it, the world isn't always perfect, but having more user-friendly, easy-to-see and -follow documents available and having our skilled operators explain how tasks should be done is simply another way to improve the culture here, helping our employees participate in the process of ongoing improvement."

Doug is officially done with the sales pitch. He has been taught in some of his executive training never to have more than three or four major points or people might forget them. But he decided to take a risk, a risk he thought was a fair one to take, and let technology create a more current look at things and hopefully help sell any idea to the team.

"I would like to say something," Mike, the Quality Manager notes, "We have discussed many different programs and fads in my 43 years here at the plant. And as Ralph Waldo Emerson once said, 'the years teach much what the days never knew.' We love to invent new buzzwords, new slogans, and new brands of manufacturing that hopefully take us into the next phase of awesome manufacturing success. I love what Todd has done by bringing in the new machines, I like what Doug has suggested regarding using video training documentation, and I love that Janice is absolutely passionate about making sure the equipment is actually running and making parts for our customers. Jamie, thank you for leading this wonderful team. Of course, the part that I play in this orchestra is the true value creation of having a management system that maintains the quality of our products. There is nothing more insightful to me that allowing my ISO management system to include a clear process for continuous improvement that maintains the use of our employees' ideas and suggestions. From all my years of manufacturing experience, I can say that a system without a control plan in place is doomed to failure. But a system designed with intent and with commitment and with rigor, is bound to achieve its goal.

ISO and Lean are far from being rivals or enemies. They are twin sisters, friends, and mutual assistants. These two sciences run into each other."

Jamie, rather silent during this description of the system by Mike and Doug, finally speaks up, "OK, team, let's move on it. I have been saying since the beginning how important our employees are to our success. As leaders, we must prove this to them. Like Bilher #1, we aren't going to expect that the system is turned on and runs. But we will make sure the process of continuous improvement is integrated in our Quality Management System. If we are allowed a buzzword for this strategy, I will offer you this rather simple one—LMS-9001."

Doug realizes that the factory people need to understand what is going on, what is changing, why it is changing, and how it will change. Step #4 is very, very important.

"OK, given this strong support, I will move forward to develop a plan to roll this out. We can use our Management of Change process. In other words, let's not do the same thing to our people again. Let's make sure we develop a plan to roll out this change and treat everyone with respect.

So, with that, everyone, let's have our second scoop," Doug announces.

The meeting ends in a sugar rush.

Actions and Discussion Points
Have some ice cream for a morning meeting
Discuss further thoughts you have on combining the systems.
Decide on a tentative date to begin a process to develop the complete plan, including roll-out and a go-live date for others to know.
Comment again on how this new synergy with the two systems into one creates common sense.

11

History Repeats Itself; Historians Repeat Each Other

Doug remembers how the first Lean Management System was rolled out at Square M's. It came from the corporate headquarters, which in and of itself was not filled with credibility or appreciation. It seemed to have been a mandate from above that theoretically sounded useful and reasonable, but that was much easier said than done. Theories of engaging all of the employees in helping improve the business and, better yet, helping them feel empowered sounded absolutely awesome. How could anyone disagree with that?!

Unfortunately, life in manufacturing is not quite so easy. Doug frequently has been shocked by how new leaders go to expensive seminars in beautiful locations, listen to extremely smooth talking consultants, and come back and tell everyone how we in manufacturing need to implement the new program. At the root of the inspiration is a very intuitive recognition that many systems have gaps or weaknesses and the communication of unique tools or ways to fill those gaps sounds like the perfect way to turn the culture into a successful top-performing organization.

Doug doesn't want the change he is suggesting in Square M's improvement process to be rolled out in the same way.

He doesn't want it to be the new flavor of the month.

He doesn't want his historian perspective on poor roll-outs to be repeated by another historian the next time. He wants good leadership to "work through" how a united team should effectively make changes. So, he decides to ask, humbly, to walk through a process of change. Why? That answer is simple—for the sake of the employees who we so eagerly want to empower and engage.

It sounds a little too obvious. But it won't repeat the same historic mistake.

Preparing for the change does take work and does create a delay in implementation.

Doug calls the first of several meetings and starts to explain, "It requires time and energy from management to be involved in making sure this improvement improves our improvement system. If anyone thinks I emphasized improvement too much, they're wrong! We need to do this respectfully and with humility. We need to do this right. If we as leaders cannot learn and improve how we roll out changes, I really doubt the people will buy into the changes."

"And, if I might add," Mike, the Quality Manager throws in, "we are actually melding the additional management system under our already existing management system... Isn't that lean?"

Only a few people laugh.

"You know I believe in helping our employees," Janice pipes in, "but we need to be aware of how most of them think about the current system. Some of the areas do reasonably well but most are not up to date, not really supported, and not at all considered much more than being three of the eight deadly wastes of lean—waiting, overprocessing, and talent. They are waiting for us to listen. We are not using their talent, and we are overprocessing information, with not enough results."

8 Deadly Sins of Waste

1 Over-Production

2 Over-Processing

3 Excess Inventory

4 Defects

5 Transportation

6 Wasted Motion

7 Waiting Time

8 Unused Employee Genius

"Speaking about humility," Doug comments, "I think that sums it up pretty well. So, with that as a great preface, I need to ask the question, 'Do we agree we need to help our organization manage the change from current state to improved future state?'"

The room is quiet.

Doug continues, "Let me explain the general flow of what I would like to do to manage the change. As we have been utilizing a system that clearly doesn't have much credibility right now, I want to walk through it slowly and clearly. I will break it down into nine steps. There are Eight Deadly Wastes in Manufacturing, but I wanted to make this process have at least one more.

The first one we have already begun to talk about. Janice put it well. We need to do what I will call an assessment of our current state and our current context. Questions like, 'What current internal and external events are taking place?' and 'Based on past actions, how are people likely to react?' Something else to think through is if we have any internal resource constraints. All of these should be part of our context assessment. I am pretty sure that if we don't do this, the 'flavor of the month' history will simply repeat itself."

"I do get your point, Doug," Jamie the Plant Manager says, "so, what is the nine-point list you're referring to?"

"OK, here it is. I think it would be worth a weekly meeting for each of these steps," Doug confidently says. Doug continues, "Let me roll out the steps of changing the Lean system development process:

1. Context Assessment—this is what we are talking about, but with a few more questions.
2. A Compelling Story—this is a form of "elevator speech" which clearly explains why we are upgrading the current system. If we can't do this, we will certainly lose our audience.
3. Stakeholder Alignment—We have to make sure we understand who all of the stakeholders are, and where they are in relation to the planned change. Once this is reviewed, we will need to determine a strategy for how each stakeholder will be explained the interest in our process change. Although this might sound like a big pain to do, I am sure doing this type of homework will certainly pay off in the long run.
4. Organizational Design—Does the organizational alignment support the change? Have the roles and responsibilities been clearly defined and communicated? Has the project team been formed, and do the members have the skills and competencies to execute the tasks?
5. Change Impacts—Is the organization prepared for the upcoming change and ready to proactively plan

appropriate actions? What risks are involved, and do we have mitigation plans for these?

6. Coach/Train/Develop—What are the key behaviors and mindsets to be changed? Will this be rolled out slow enough to properly manage the coaching and training? What training is required? Are the trainers available?

7. Change Implementation—What change activities are required to activate and support this transformation?

8. Sustain and Anticipate—How will success be measured? What are leading indicators? Will we ask our people to review what they think of the change? Have we told them we will be asking them to give us feedback?

9. Readiness, Communication, and Measurement— Have all impacted individuals been informed? Do we have sufficient time and resources to take on all this training so it is done right this time? Are key stakeholders committed to the change? Have we effectively communicated the elevator speech and filled in any specifics that people will ask? Do we definitely have a two-way communication plan in place for this upcoming change? How will we follow up and make sure we as leaders stay committed to this change, based on the employees' impact?

So, let's be honest with each other. Changing a process that is intended to engage and empower our entire workforce is simply not a 'put up a board with columns and go' process. It will require excellent leadership, excellent support of our teams, and actually going out to the floor where the work gets done to coach and communicate what is being done about their suggestions and ideas."

Doug suddenly wonders if he might have said too much. But he isn't ashamed. He really needs full support, and he is clearly rolling out the change process, which is intended not to repeat history.

Jamie then says, "I agree with Doug. Let's make this happen—efficiently and effectively. And, I might add, with a humble attitude. Doug has brought up, in a rather respectful way, our part in the condition of the current Lean Management System weaknesses. Let's do it right this time."

Actions and Discussion Points
For those who have been through several iterations of Lean Management Systems in their careers, consider how a change might be received
Schedule out the 9 Step Process. Decide on a date to begin the process to develop the complete plan including roll-out and a Go-Live Date for others to know
Ask the Lean Manager to develop a small team that will create templates/worksheets for each step, if not already available.
Comment on how this new commitment to change management creates common sense. Is there any part of it doesn't create common sense?

12

Excellence in Leadership

Six months later, Doug contemplates the joy of walking through the process of ongoing improvement for the, pardon the repetition, on-going improvement process. He has everything he wanted in a system.

Common sense.

Accountability.

Nice technology.

Changes that are frequently connected and managed directly through the already established standards.

Everyone on the leadership team on the same page.

One and only one sustainable system.

Excellent high-potential employees getting trained on how to foster success.

Lean process audits that are coaching people on the value of the ISO documentation and how they work together.

No frustration.

No buzzwords, except one—LMS-9001.

The daily grind is still real. Bilher #1 still goes down. Janice still gets excited. Todd is still self-confident. Mike is still calm and methodical.

And Doug?

He's passionately supporting and enjoying working with the certified trainers, addressing the gaps between what they are learning and what the management team should be providing, and continuing to enjoy the daily dishwashing OEE improvements.

Index

V

VDM, 2–3
Visual communication process
     requirements, 48–49

W

Washing/rinsing process, 35

For Product Safety Concerns and Information please contact our EU representative GPSR@taylorandfrancis.com Taylor & Francis Verlag GmbH, Kaufingerstraße 24, 80331 München, Germany

T - #0034 - 230425 - C0 - 203/133/6 [8] - CB - 9780367137151 - Gloss Lamination